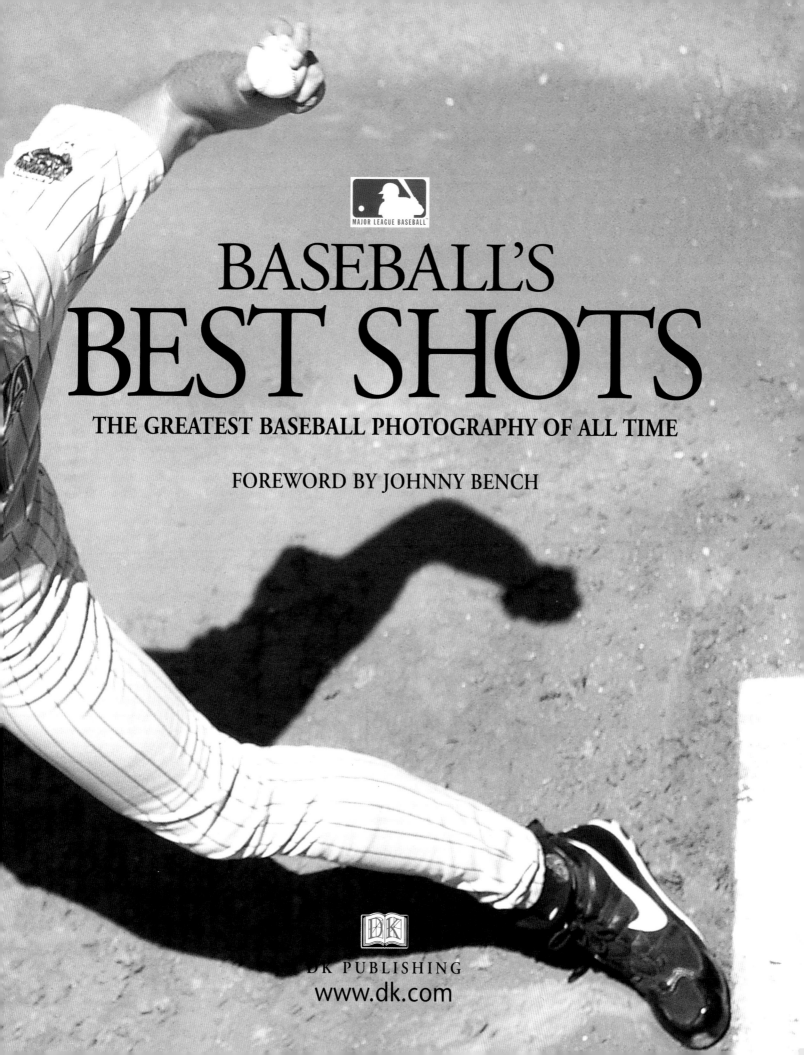

BASEBALL'S BEST SHOTS

THE GREATEST BASEBALL PHOTOGRAPHY OF ALL TIME

FOREWORD BY JOHNNY BENCH

DK PUBLISHING
www.dk.com

BASEBALL'S BEST SHOTS

THE GREATEST BASEBALL PHOTOGRAPHY OF ALL TIME

 Dorling Kindersley

 MAJOR LEAGUE BASEBALL

Editor, Beth Adelman
Designer, Timothy Shaner
Publisher, Sean Moore
Editorial Director, LaVonne Carlson

Foreword Assistance, Vanessa-Juliana Petker

DK Publishing, Inc.
375 Hudson Street
New York, New York 10014

Timothy J. Brosnan, Executive Vice President
Don Hintze, Director of Publishing and MLB Photos
Rich Pilling, Manager, MLB Photos
Paul Cunningham, Administrator, MLB Photos

Major League Baseball Properties, Inc.
245 Park Avenue
New York, NY 10167

DK Publishing, Inc. offers special discounts for bulk purchases for sales promotions or
premiums. Specific, large-quantity needs can be met with special editions, including personalized covers,
excerpts of existing guides, and corporate imprints. For more information, contact Special Markets Department,
DK Publishing, Inc., 375 Hudson Street, New York, NY 10014   Fax: 212-689-5254.

First Paperback Edition, 2002
1 2 4 6 8 10 9 7 5 3

Library of Congress Cataloging -in-Publication Data
Baseball's best shots.--1st Paperback ed.
p. cm
ISBN 0-7894-8915-5
1. Baseball--United States--Pictorial works. 2. Baseball players--United
States--Pictorial works. I. Dorling Kindersley Publishing, Inc.
GV867.4 .B28 2000
796.357--dc21   00-030691

Color reproduction by Colourpath, London, England
Printed and bound by Toppan Printing Company, Ltd., China

see our complete product line at
www.dk.com

PURE JOY
(PAGE 1)
SCOTT BROSIUS OF THE NEW YORK
YANKEES CELEBRATES AFTER THE FINAL
OUT OF THE 1998 WORLD SERIES
AGAINST THE SAN DIEGO PADRES.
BROSIUS WAS NAMED SERIES MVP.
PHOTO BY RON VESELY/MLB PHOTOS, 1998

A LONG STRETCH
(PAGE 2)
RANDY JOHNSON OF THE ARIZONA
DIAMONDBACKS IS PROBABLY BASEBALL'S
MOST INTIMIDATING LEFT-HANDER.
AT 6-FOOT-10, HE'S PROBABLY ALSO
THE TALLEST PLAYER EVER.
PHOTO BY JON SOOHOO

IN THE GLARE ➤
JOE DIMAGGIO WORE THESE FLIP-UP
SUNGLASSES TO CUT THE GLARE IN
THE OUTFIELD. THIS PHOTO WAS
TAKEN DURING HIS FAMOUS HITTING
STREAK, WHEN DIMAGGIO HIT IN
56 CONSECUTIVE GAMES.
PHOTO BY ASSOCIATED PRESS, 1941

FOREWORD

BY JOHNNY BENCH

I t is said that one picture is worth a thousand words, but can you imagine it being worth about 100 miles an hour? That's the speed of Nolan Ryan's pitch as it's travelling up to the man at home plate. Many of you will not experience the intensity of expectation like this, but through the eyes and skills of a photographer, this moment has been preserved for you to wonder at.

Baseball's Best Shots has been an exhaustive journey of selecting the best photographs taken of the game of baseball. There are millions of photos within the files of the Major League ballclubs and the portfolios of 150 years worth of photographers. How can it be that only a select few have been chosen for this book? The words we use to describe these eloquent images offer a clue. When proposing words to attach to a photo, which would you choose? Endurance? It's the word that is scrawled upon the faces of Hack Wilson and Babe Ruth. Grace? You can see it in Derek Jeter's body as he takes flight to throw for the double play. Turn to page 105 for Comradeship and Respect as you catch both McGwire and Sosa on first base. Their race, although one of historic value, was also one of Respect and Honor.

There is Mischief and Humor, too. Catch a preview of this on page 126, from the great Babe and Lou Gehrig. Simplicity is also a criterion of a good photo. Dan Donovan caught this kind of beauty on film with his photo of the wooden bats and their carved numbers on page 70, all awaiting their chance at bat.

What else makes a great photograph? My eye immediately noticed the technical aspects of the triple exposure on page 54 of David Cone as he proceeds into the pitch – truly an art captured in slow motion. The shadow on page 158 demonstrates the photographer's navigation of his own body, the manipulation of the natural light surrounding the field, and the lenses he chose in order to make this great image.

The photos selected here are those that can bring your senses alive. Perhaps you too can feel the stickiness of the pine as you grip the bat and the sweat trickling down your cheeks as your heart thuds in your chest while you anticipate the release of the baseball from the pitcher's fingertips. Or perhaps you can see the play in slow motion – the baseball suspended in air, the pitcher's hand and torso falling forward from gravity. Your ears pick up the crack of hide hitting wood, the dirt scuffed up into the air as the players' cleats push out toward first base. A call at first, a slide at second, and a home run batted in – it all happens so fast to our naked eye. It's only through the stopped motion of the camera that we have the opportunity to feel the drama of the skills of a Major League ball player.

Since 1869, the games played have produced memories that cannot be forgotten. The men who have made this game great are from all walks of life and all have contributed to our American heritage – whether it's the player who only got one hit, or Pete Rose's 4,256 hits, or Hank Aaron's 755 home runs. This book depicts the determination and desire that lives in the heart of every man who has ever worn a Major League uniform. This book also portrays the love of the game beheld by the men who have used their artistic eye to capture the silent eloquence of baseball.

There are moments of baseball that live like photos in my mind. Every detail is still vivid and the feelings are strong. I can see myself sitting with Dad on the couch with a half-gallon of Neapolitan ice cream, watching the games on TV. Dad's voice would boom out, "I could hit that guy." Then, as the next pitcher positioned himself on the mound, I would hear the familiar voice once again, "I could hit that guy," and again, "I could hit that guy – and that guy too." The first time I faced Bob Gibson, my bat saw three strikes and a lot of air. As I walked back to the dugout smiling, the manager asked, "What's so funny?" I thought to myself, "I don't think Dad could hit this guy!"

Mickey Mantle, Ty Cobb, Honus Wagner, Hack Wilson, Satchel Paige, the Babe, and the Iron Horse – I played their game but I never got to shake their hands or see them play with my own eyes. It's a loss for you and me, but time stands still through these photos and we have the privilege to revisit these men again and again.

Every man, woman, and child who picks up this book may not be a ballplayer, but we all have the opportunity to experience the game of baseball through these photos. A worthy cry of praise is due to the photographers who made the effort to immortalize these men and the intrigue of baseball. And so, do not wait any longer; let your fingers turn these pages of instants in time and in art. As you do, think about which words you would choose for each photo. As your eye absorbs the photo, count up the words. Do you come up with more than a thousand? Enjoy the journey!

JOHNNY BENCH TALKS THINGS OVER WITH CINCINNATI REDS MANAGER SPARKY ANDERSON. THE REDS WERE KNOWN AS THE BIG RED MACHINE, AND WON THE WORLD SERIES THE YEAR THIS PHOTO WAS TAKEN. PHOTO BY TONY TOMSIC/MLB PHOTOS, 1976

Johnny Bench was born in Oklahoma on December 7, 1947. His childhood dream was to become a Major League Baseball player and his father told him being a catcher was the most direct route to that goal. Taking that advice, he was selected in the 1965 amateur draft by the Cincinnati Reds and signed with them. Bench made Cincinnati's Major League roster for the 1968 season. This marked the beginning of one of the most successful careers in baseball history. Elected to the Baseball Hall of Fame in January 1989, Bench is undoubtedly the greatest catcher ever, and was named to the All-Century Team as starting catcher. His honors include National League Rookie of the Year (1968), National League MVP (1970 and 1972), World Series MVP (1976), 14-time All-Star, and 10 Gold Glove Awards. In 1980, Bench set an endurance record by catching 100 or more games for 13 consecutive seasons. He maintains a sense of balance by using his celebrity status to aid worthy causes, such as the Heart Association, the American Cancer Society (as past National Chairman of Athletes vs. Cancer), the Kidney Foundation, Franciscan Sisters of the Poor, the American Lung Association, and the "Catch the Cure" program of the Children's Hospital on Cincinnati. He also supports the Cincinnati Symphony, the Museum of Science and Industry, and his own Johnny Bench Scholarship Fund, which grants financial aid to Cincinnati college students.

INTRODUCTION

BY RICH PILLING AND PAUL CUNNINGHAM

Picking the greatest photography of Major League Baseball is a daunting task. For this book, we were asked to distill nearly 150 years of baseball photography into a compilation of 124 great photographs. Inevitably, the results are bound to spark debate, just like selecting the best home run hitter, the top all-around player, or the nastiest slider of all time.

Baseball's history is part of the fabric of America. Many people remember dramatic moments that recall the nostalgia of their youth or players that seem to define an era. And so much of baseball's history has been documented photographically. Some historic moments have made great photographs, but a great photograph is not necessarily an historic moment. So rather than try to make this book a pictorial history of baseball, we sought to showcase some of the best baseball photographers from the twentieth century. Men with a passion for the game, but also an artistic eye. We also wanted to depict aspects of the game, apart from the players, that illuminate the romance of baseball.

The search was exhaustive. The staff of the National Baseball Hall of Fame in Cooperstown, particularly Pat Kelly, Bill Burdick, and Milo Stewart in the Hall's Photo Library, gave us invaluable assistance in finding historical images. Tom Shieber, also at the Hall of Fame, was an important source of information. Many of the world's most accomplished baseball photographers were asked to submit their best material, and the files of Major League Baseball Photos were searched up and down for contenders.

There are a host of criteria that were considered before deeming an image worthy of being a Best Shot. On page 18, Nat Fein's shot of Babe Ruth's farewell at Yankee Stadium won a Pulitzer Prize for photography in 1949. That was good enough for us. Babe Ruth's exuberance seemed to personify America's mood during the roaring twenties. Fein's image, taken on June 13, 1948, captured the sad farewell to an American icon. Fein is alive and well, and with little prompting he will recount the details of the day he shot this famous photo. He will tell you about an ailing Ruth being helped into his Yankee uniform before taking the field. Fein even recalls that the bat Ruth was leaning on was not his own, but one he had borrowed from Cleveland Indians pitcher Bob Feller – himself a Hall of Famer.

Unusual elements can contribute to the making of a great photograph. An example is Bill Stover's image on page 24. It was taken at Busch Stadium in St. Louis. The image relies on repeated arches to illustrate its theme. When you first look at the photo, you notice arch-shaped shadows cast on the playing field, then you notice the arches as part of the architectural details of the stadium. In the background, towering over the city is the St. Louis Gateway Arch. And a natural arch, a rainbow, dominates the scene, justifying this image's worthiness as a Best Shot.

Sometimes lady luck and autofocus cameras play a role in the creation of a Best Shot. An example of this is the photo of Mitch Williams on page 89. Ron Vesely was covering the 1993 World Series between the Philadelphia Phillies and the Toronto Blue Jays. In one of the most dramatic finishes of all time, Joe Carter hit a last-at-bat, come-from-behind, World Series-clinching home run off Williams. Vesely captured Carter's home run swing, and then, as he prepared to shoot his jubilant trip around the bases, Williams walked into the frame. Ron's camera, with a mind of its own, decided to focus on Williams instead of Carter. The result is a brilliant photograph; dejected Williams in focus in the foreground, jubilant Carter, out of focus but clearly visible in the background. In one image, the thrill of victory and the agony of defeat converge.

What else makes a great photograph? Some of the images feature dramatic lighting, such as Brad Mangin's shot of Dwight Gooden on page 153. Others feature dramatic action captured at its peak, like Dean Palmer diving for the ball on page 20, taken by John Williamson. Some images reflect the competitive nature of the players by capturing intense facial expressions, such as Charles M. Conlon's famous shot of Ty Cobb sliding into third base on page 64. Others are the execution of an artistic vision, like John Reid III's fan shot on page 33.

When the game begins, there are many positions a photographer can shoot from. Best Shots often show ordinary action captured from an unusual perspective. Michael Zagaris' photo of Ben Grieve on page 78 clearly illustrates the aesthetic value of shooting from a different perspective.

For a photographer, one of the pleasures of photographing baseball is the infinite elements of the game that lend themselves to great pictures. The baseball photographer with an artistic eye is never short of subjects: the personalities of the game captured in portrait form; the candid, joyful images of men playing a boy's game. Creatively photographed baseball equipment – the balls, bats, and gloves – can speak volumes about the romance of the game. Stadiums themselves, green cathedrals packed with screaming fans, are some of the most dramatic photo subjects. Baseball differs from almost every other sport in that each ballpark is dramatically

different. The infield itself is consistent, but that's where the similarities end. Some parks have deep fences and wide foul territory, seemingly designed to keep the pitchers happy. Other parks, with their short porches and odd angles, cater to the hitters. Photography illustrates each park's uniqueness, frozen in time for all eyes to marvel.

The following pages are the distillation – our picks for baseball's Best Shots. Some of these photos you may have seen before. Some just tickled our fancy. Of the thousands of images that were considered, we think these are the best.

Rich Pilling is the Manager and Paul Cunningham is the Administrator of Major League Baseball Photos. They have a combined total of 36 years of experience in the photographic community.

ME NEXT
MARK MCGWIRE SIGNS AUTOGRAPHS
FOR HIS FANS AT BUSCH STADIUM
IN ST. LOUIS BEFORE A GAME.
PHOTO BY DAN DONOVAN/MLB PHOTOS, 1998

◄ WHAT A KICK
New York Yankee Orlando "El Duque" Hernandez
in action against the San Diego Padres in
the World Series. That high kick, developed
in his native Cuba, is a unique part of
El Duque's delivery.
Photo by V.J. Lovero/Sports Illustrated, 1998

◣ PERFECT BALANCE
Warren Spahn of the Boston Braves shows a
completely different, and equally precarious
pitching style. Spahn is the winningest left-
hander of all time. This picture was taken
during Spring Training his rookie year.
Photo by Associated Press, 1942

QUICK TURN

Andy Fox, Arizona Diamondbacks shortstop,
gets Jeff Blauser of the Chicago Cubs out at
second and looks to turn the double play.
Photo by Bob Rosato/MLB Photos, 1998

◁ EXCLAMATION POINT

JUAN ENCARNACION OF THE DETROIT TIGERS AT
BAT AGAINST THE ST. LOUIS CARDINALS.
PHOTO BY V.J. LOVERO/SPORTS ILLUSTRATED, 1999

△ GREASE IT UP

BURLEIGH GRIMES OF THE CHICAGO CUBS WAS THE
LAST OF THE LEGAL SPITBALLERS. HERE HE DEMON-
STRATES HIS TECHNIQUE FOR GREASING THE BALL.
PHOTO BY NATIONAL BASEBALL LIBRARY, 1932-33

LAST GOODBYE

THIS WAS GEORGE HERMAN "BABE" RUTH'S LAST
APPEARANCE AT YANKEE STADIUM BEFORE HIS
DEATH FROM CANCER IN 1948. THE BAMBINO IS
BEST KNOWN FOR HITTING 714 HOMERUNS IN
HIS CAREER, AND FOR INFUSING THE GAME
WITH HIS LARGER-THAN-LIFE PERSONALITY.
THIS PHOTO WON A PULITZER PRIZE.
PHOTO BY NAT FEIN, 1948

STRETCH AND CATCH
DEAN PALMER OF THE KANSAS
CITY ROYALS SNARES A BALL AT THIRD.
PHOTO BY JOHN WILLIAMSON/MLB PHOTOS, 1998

GAME FACE
Lewis Robert "Hack" Wilson played outfield
for the Chicago Cubs from 1926 to 1931.
He holds the record for most RBI's in a
single season, driving 190 men home in 1930.
Photo by National Baseball Library/MLB Photos

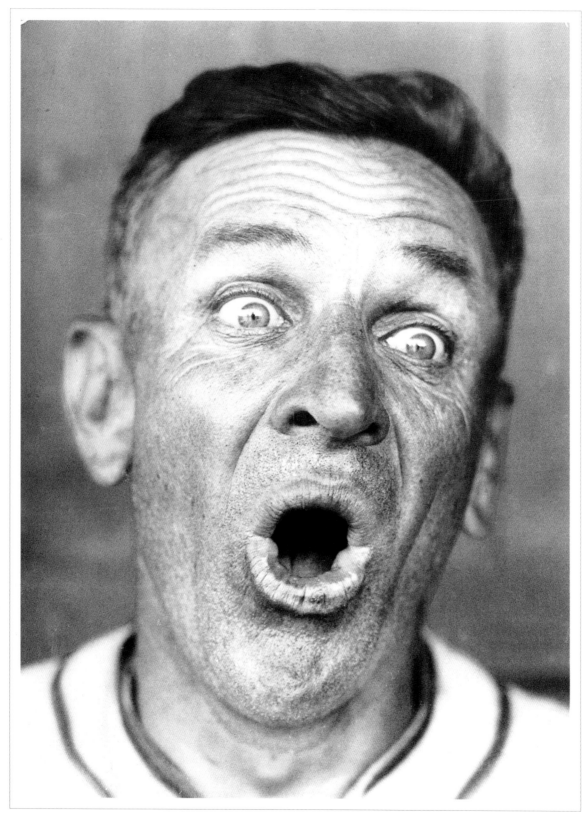

CLOWN FACE

CHARLES DILLON "CASEY" STENGEL BEGAN HIS CAREER IN THE
MAJORS IN 1912 PLAYING FOR THE BROOKLYN DODGERS, AND ENDED
IT IN 1965 MANAGING THE NEW YORK METS. IN BETWEEN HE MANAGED
THE YANKEES TO 10 PENNANTS IN 12 YEARS (1949-1960).
PHOTO BY NATIONAL BASEBALL LIBRARY/MLB PHOTOS

◄ OPENING DAY

THIS IS OPENING DAY OF A MAGICAL SEASON IN
BUSCH STADIUM, ST. LOUIS, AND ALL THE ARCHES
ARE ALIGNED – FROM THE SHADOWS ON THE FIELD
TO THE ARCHITECTURE IN THE STADIUM TO THE
ST. LOUIS ARCH TO THE RAINBOW ABOVE IT ALL.
PHOTO BY BILL STOVER/MLB PHOTOS, 1998

OPENING DAY ▲

THIS IS OPENING DAY AT THE NEW YANKEE STADIUM,
KNOWN AS THE HOUSE THAT RUTH BUILT. AND IT
WAS TRUE; THE REVENUE BABE RUTH BROUGHT IN
ENABLED THE TEAM TO BUILD THE NEW BALLPARK
IN THE BRONX. PREVIOUSLY, THE YANKEES
PLAYED AT THE POLO GROUNDS IN MANHATTAN.
PHOTO BY NATIONAL BASEBALL LIBRARY/MLB PHOTOS, 1923

ARABESQUE
DEREK JETER OF THE NEW YORK YANKEES
TURNS A DOUBLE PLAY FROM SECOND BASE.
PHOTO BY RICH PILLING/MLB PHOTOS, 1996

⋀ TOOLS OF THE TRADE
THE GLOVE AND SUNGLASSES OF
OUTFIELDER HAROLD BAINES OF THE
CHICAGO WHITE SOX. THE FLIP SHADES
AREN'T MUCH DIFFERENT FROM THE
ONES JOE DIMAGGIO WEARS ON PAGE 5.
PHOTO BY RICH PILLING/MLB PHOTOS, 1984

GREAT START ➤
MARK MCGWIRE IS ON HIS HOME RUN TROT
AFTER HITTING A GRAND SLAM ON OPENING
DAY AT BUSCH STADIUM. IT SET THE TONE
FOR HIS RECORD-BREAKING SEASON.
PHOTO BY DAN DONOVAN/MLB PHOTOS, 1998

THE SWING

THIS IS WHAT THE UMPIRE SEES
WHEN SAMMY SOSA OF THE
CHICAGO CUBS WHACKS ONE.
PHOTO BY ROBERT BECK/MLB PHOTOS

≺ BUNT AND RUN

OZZIE SMITH OF THE ST. LOUIS
CARDINALS LAYS DOWN A BUNT IN FRONT
OF MARK PARENT OF THE CHICAGO CUBS.
PHOTO BY DAN DONOVAN, 1994

LET'S GO! ⋏

FANS AT YANKEE STADIUM ENJOY THE
WORLD SERIES BETWEEN NEW YORK
AND THE SAN DIEGO PADRES.
PHOTO BY JOHN REID III/MLB PHOTOS, 1998

SPRING CLEANING
Before the season starts,
the seats are spruced up
for Colorado Rockies fans.
Photo by Eric Lars Bakke/MLB Photos

WET ⋏
ST. LOUIS CARDINALS OUTFIELDER ENOS
SLAUGHTER IS DRENCHED WITH SWEAT
AFTER A HARD WORKOUT DURING SPRING
TRAINING IN ST. PETERSBURG, FLORIDA. HE
WAS 35 AT THE TIME, AND SAID, "US OLD
BOYS HAVE TO WORK TO GET INTO SHAPE."
PHOTO BY ASSOCIATED PRESS, 1951

AND WETTER ➤
CHICAGO CUBS OUTFIELDER SAMMY SOSA
KEEPS COOL DURING HIS RECORD-BREAKING
SEASON BY THROWING WATER IN HIS FACE.
PHOTO BY RICH PILLING/MLB PHOTOS, 1998

RIGHT DOWN THE LINE ⌃
TRAVIS FRYMAN OF THE CLEVELAND
INDIANS FOULS A BALL UP THE THIRD BASE
LINE AND ALMOST HITS HIS TEAMMATE ON
THIRD, WHO DANCES OUT OF THE WAY.
PHOTO BY JOHN REID III/MLB PHOTOS, 1998

IN THE POCKET ➤
THE BALL IS ON ITS WAY INTO THE
DEEP GLOVE OF THIS CATCHER,
SET IN THE CLASSIC CROUCH.
PHOTO BY RON VESELY

SAY HEY ⋏

A YOUNG WILLIE MAYS PLAYS HERE FOR THE NEW YORK
GIANTS. HALL OF FAMER MAYS' STAGGERING CAREER
STATISTICS INCLUDE 3,283 HITS, 660 HOME RUNS AND
A .302 AVERAGE. HE ACCUMULATED 12 GOLD GLOVES,
AND PLAYED IN A RECORD-TYING 24 ALL-STAR GAMES.
PHOTO BY DON WINGFIELD/THE PERFECT PICTURE

SAY YEA ➢

A FAN IN A CALIFORNIA ANGELS CAP
HOLDS UP A SMALL BASEBALL CARD.
PHOTO BY KIRK SCHLEA

PLAY AT THE PLATE
Chris Stynes of the Cincinnati Reds
jars the ball loose from catcher
Mike Redmond of the Florida Marlins.
Photo by Tom Dipace, 1998

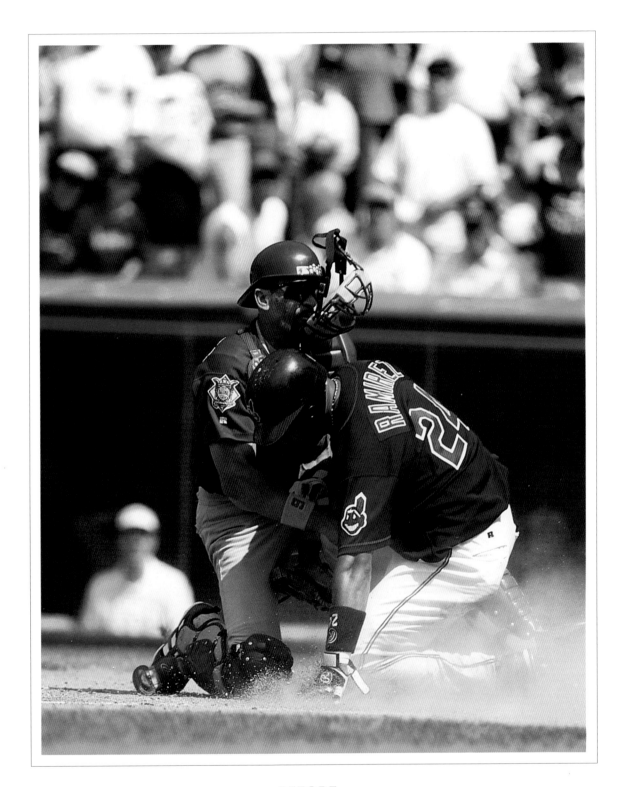

BEFORE...

MANNY RAMIREZ OF THE CLEVELAND INDIANS
COLLIDES WITH CHICAGO CUBS CATCHER
BENITO SANTIAGO. THE BALL WAS JUST THROWN
TO SANTIAGO BY SAMMY SOSA IN RIGHT FIELD.
PHOTO BY JOHN GRIESHOP/MLB PHOTOS, 1999

…AND AFTER

THIS BONE-CRUNCHING COLLISION TOOK PLACE
DURING AN INTERLEAGUE GAME IN CLEVELAND.
PHOTO BY JOHN GRIESHOP/MLB PHOTOS, 1999

◁ FANATIC
FANS OF SAN DIEGO PADRES
CLOSER TREVOR HOFFMAN MAKE
THEIR FEELINGS KNOWN DURING
GAME 3 OF THE WORLD SERIES.
PHOTO BY BOB ROSATO/MLB PHOTOS, 1998

ARE YOU BLIND? ⊼
TOMMY LaSORDA OF THE LOS ANGELES
DODGERS MAKES HIS POINT TO
UMPIRE BRUCE FROEMMING.
PHOTO BY RON VESELY

CHEAP SEATS ➤

Fans enjoy the Hall of Fame Game in Cooperstown, New York. An exhibition game is always played at Doubleday Field on the Monday following the induction ceremonies.
Photo by Philip Kamrass/Albany Times Union, 1999

COMING AND GOING

(Previous Page)

Welder Henman Ross works on the new Miller Park, while across the street a Milwaukee Brewers game is being played at the old County Stadium.
Photo by Dale Guldan/Milwaukee Journal Sentinel, 1998

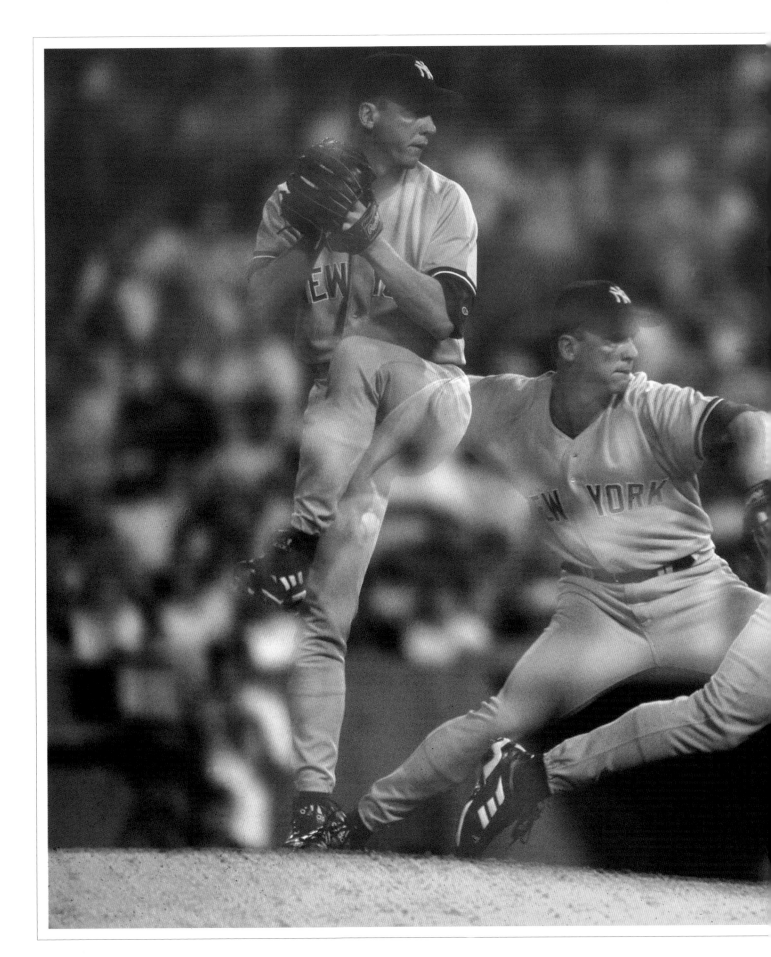

◁ THE WINDUP

NEW YORK YANKEE DAVID CONE
SHOWS HIS PITCHING FORM
IN THIS MULTIPLE EXPOSURE.
PHOTO BY V.J. LOVERO/SPORTS
ILLUSTRATED

WORK THAT BODY

(PREVIOUS PAGE)
THE OAKLAND A'S WORK OUT DURING
SPRING TRAINING AT PHOENIX
MUNICIPAL STADIUM.
PHOTO BY RICH PILLING/MLB
PHOTOS, 1994

⋀ LIGHT IT UP
FIREWORKS OVER BUSCH STADIUM
IN ST. LOUIS.
PHOTO BY DAN DONOVAN/MLB PHOTOS

FUTURE HALL OF FAMER ➤
THE DETROIT TIGERS FATHER-SON GAME.
PHOTO BY LOUIS DELUCA

HIT ME!
(PREVIOUS PAGE)
THE NOTORIOUS BLEACHER CROWD AT
CHICAGO'S WRIGLEY FIELD CHEERS ON
SAMMY SOSA DURING HIS FAMOUS HOME
RUN DUEL WITH MARK MCGWIRE. SOSA
ENDED UP WITH 66 HOME RUNS THAT
SEASON AND MCGWIRE WITH 70, BOTH
BREAKING ROGER MARIS' RECORD OF 61.
PHOTO BY DAVID DUROCHIK/MLB PHOTOS, 1998

A DIP IN THE POOL?
SPRING RAINS FLOODED THE MIDWEST,
TURNING MILWAUKEE COUNTY STADIUM
INTO A SWIMMING POOL. THIS PHOTO
WAS TAKEN ON JUNE 20.
PHOTO BY JOE PICCIOLO/MLB PHOTOS, 1997

RAIN DELAY ➤
THE GROUNDS CREW FOR THE KANSAS
CITY ROYALS PULLS OUT THE RAIN
TARP TO COVER THE INFIELD.
PHOTO BY JOHN KLEIN/MLB PHOTOS

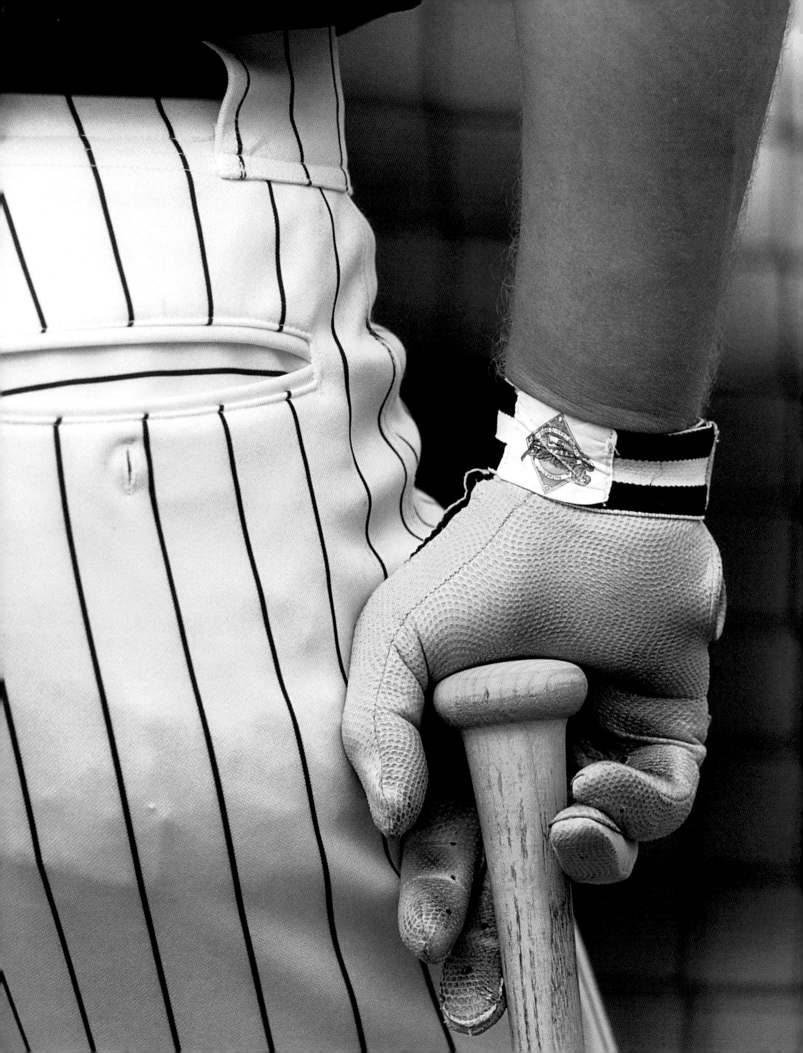

◁ LEAN ON ME

SPRING TRAINING AT THE
COLORADO ROCKIES CAMP.
PHOTO BY ERIC LARS BAKKE

GET ON THE BUS ⋏

THE OAKLAND A'S TEAM BUS DURING
SPRING TRAINING IN MESA, ARIZONA.
THAT'S A YOUNG MARK MCGWIRE
IN THE LEFT CENTER.
PHOTO BY MICHAEL ZAGARIS, 1988

THE SLIDE

ONE OF THE MOST FAMOUS BASEBALL PHOTOS
OF ALL TIME IS THIS PICTURE OF TY COBB
OF THE DETROIT TIGERS STEALING THIRD
OFF NEW YORK HIGHLANDER JIMMY AUSTIN.
AS THE PHOTOGRAPHER SAW IT, "TY NEVER
DELIBERATELY SPIKES A PLAYER, I BELIEVE.
BUT HE DOES INSIST ON HIS RIGHT TO THE
BASE PATHS, WHICH IS PROPER."
PHOTO BY CHARLES M. CONLON/THE SPORTING
NEWS, 1909

PRECARIOUS PRIZE
A FAN AT FORBES FIELD IN PITTSBURGH REACHES
FOR A FOUL BALL DURING GAME 2 OF THE WORLD
SERIES. THE PITTSBURGH PIRATES EVENTUALLY
BEAT THE NEW YORK YANKEES IN GAME 7, WHEN
BILL MAZEROSKI HIT A DRAMATIC HOME RUN
IN THE BOTTOM OF THE NINTH INNING.
PHOTO BY NATIONAL BASEBALL LIBRARY, 1960

HE'S PERFECT

DAVID CONE'S YANKEE TEAMMATES CELEBRATE
AFTER HE PITCHED A PERFECT GAME AGAINST THE
MONTREAL EXPOS. ONE OF THE RAREST FEATS IN
BASEBALL, IN A PERFECT GAME EVERY BATTER IS
RETIRED WITHOUT EVER REACHING BASE.
PHOTO BY KATHY WILLENS/ASSOCIATED PRESS, 1999

BOXING MATCH

MARK MCGWIRE, PLAYING FOR THE OAKLAND
A'S, IS OUT AT THE PLATE AS TORONTO BLUE
JAYS CATCHER PAT BORDERS HOLDS ONTO
THE BALL DURING THE AMERICAN LEAGUE
CHAMPIONSHIP SERIES.
PHOTO BY BRAD MANGIN/MLB PHOTOS, 1992

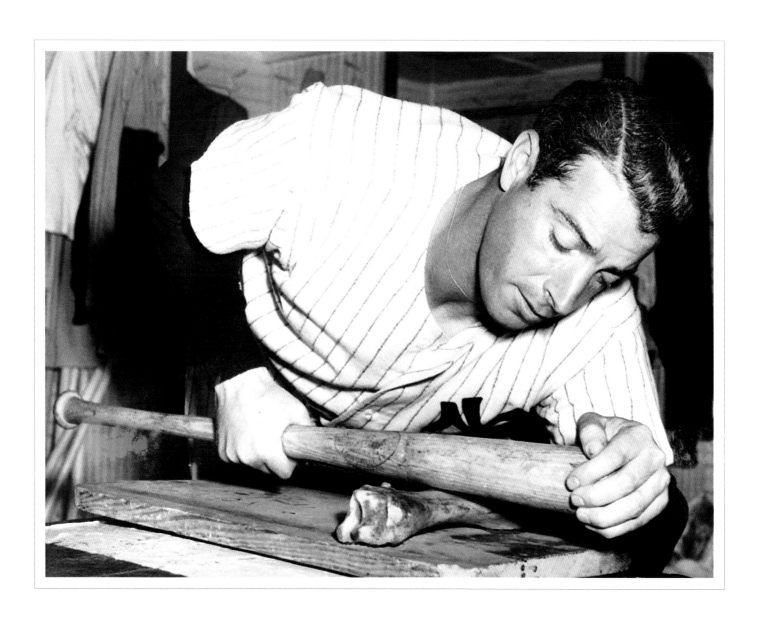

◄ WHO'S UP NEXT?

THE LARGE NUMBER MARKED ON
THE END OF THE BAT IS THE UNIFORM
NUMBER OF THE PLAYER WHO USES IT.
PHOTO BY DAN DONOVAN/MLB PHOTOS, 1998

BONING THE BAT ◢

NEW YORK YANKEE JOE DIMAGGIO RUBS HIS
BAT ACROSS A LARGE BEEF BONE. CALLED
BONING THE BAT, IT COMPRESSED THE GRAIN
OF THE WOOD TO MAKE THE BAT HARDER SO IT
WOULD LAST LONGER. LONG A COMMON PRACTICE,
PLAYERS TODAY GENERALLY SKIP THE BONING.
PHOTO BY ASSOCIATED PRESS, 1950

A QUIET MOMENT
SHORTSTOP HONUS WAGNER, KNOWN AS
"THE FLYING DUTCHMAN," PLAYED FROM 1897
TO 1917. HE SPENT MOST OF HIS CAREER
WITH THE NATIONAL LEAGUE PITTSBURGH
PIRATES. WAGNER WAS CHOSEN FOR
THE ALL-CENTURY TEAM.
PHOTO BY NATIONAL BASEBALL LIBRARY/MLB PHOTOS

A WALK IN THE WOODS
(PREVIOUS PAGE)
THIS ATLANTA BRAVES BULLPEN CATCHER
HAS NO TIME TO ENJOY THE SCENERY
IN THE BULLPEN AT COORS FIELD IN
DENVER, COLORADO.
PHOTO BY KARL GEHRING/MLB PHOTOS, 1997

△ PICK OFF
TEXAS RANGERS CATCHER IVAN RODRIGUEZ
TRIES TO THROW OUT A RUNNER.
PHOTO BY JOHN WILLIAMSON/MLB PHOTOS, 1997

STILL SPRY ⚜

Hall of Famer Connie Mack began his career
as a catcher but made his mark as a manager.
He assumed control of the Philadelphia
Athletics in 1901 and continued for
50 years until he retired at age 88.
Photo by Associated Press

◁ PLAYING THE ANGLES

THIS IS A DIFFERENT WAY TO LOOK
AT BEN GRIEVE OF THE OAKLAND A'S
SNAGGING A BALL IN RIGHT FIELD.
PHOTO BY MICHAEL ZAGARIS/MLB PHOTOS, 1998

△ PERFECT BACKDROP

RICKY HENDERSON OF THE OAKLAND A'S
MAKES A COLORFUL CATCH DURING SPRING
TRAINING IN PHOENIX, ARIZONA.
PHOTO BY BRAD MANGIN/MLB PHOTOS, 1992

LOW TAG
Luis Alicea of the St. Louis
Cardinals tags Eric Young of the
Colorado Rockies at second base.
Photo by Eric Lars Bakke, 1996

⌃ THE SULTAN OF SWAT
BABE RUTH PLAYED OUTFIELD FOR THE NEW
YORK YANKEES FROM 1920 TO 1934. HE SET A
NUMBER OF IMPORTANT RECORDS DURING THOSE
GOLDEN YEARS, INCLUDING MOST TOTAL BASES
IN A SEASON (457) AND HIGHEST SLUGGING
PERCENTAGE FOR A SEASON (.847), BOTH SET
IN 1920. IN 1927 HE HIT 60 HOME RUNS, A
RECORD THAT STOOD UNTIL ROGER MARIS HIT
61 IN 1961. HE RETIRED FROM THE BOSTON
BRAVES IN 1935 WITH 714 CAREER HOME RUNS.
PHOTO BY CHARLES M. CONLON/THE SPORTING NEWS

THE LOOK ➤
KEN CAMINITI OF THE SAN DIEGO
PADRES. CAMINITI PLAYED THIRD BASE
FOR SAN DIEGO FROM 1995 TO 1998.
PHOTO BY KIRK SCHLEA, 1995

COMING AT YOU
FOUR-TIME CY YOUNG AWARD WINNER
GREG MADDUX OF THE ATLANTA
BRAVES FACES ANOTHER BATTER.
PHOTO BY KIRK SCHLEA, 1994

THE SHOT FROM FIRST BASE
CRAIG BIGGIO OF THE HOUSTON ASTROS LOOKS
TO TURN A DOUBLE PLAY AT SECOND BASE,
AFTER TAKING A FLORIDA MARLIN IN THE GUT.
PHOTO BY DAVID BLANK/MLB PHOTOS, 1997

THE SHOT FROM THIRD BASE
A DIFFERENT PERSPECTIVE ON
THE EXACT SAME MOMENT.
PHOTO BY BOB ROSATO/MLB PHOTOS, 1997

HURTS SO BAD ⋀
As the Cleveland Indians lose Game 6 and the
World Series to the Atlanta Braves, relief
pitcher Julian Tavarez is lost in grief.
Photo by Stephen Green/MLB Photos, 1995

IT CUTS BOTH WAYS ➤
Philadelphia Phillies pitcher Mitch
Williams walks off the field in despair as
a jubilant Toronto Blue Jay Joe Carter
starts his trip around the bases after
clinching the World Series with a home
run in the bottom of the ninth in Game 6.
Photo by Ron Vesely/MLB Photos, 1993

◄ SHATTERED

ALEX GONZALEZ OF THE TORONTO
BLUE JAYS BREAKS HIS BAT ON
IMPACT WITH THE BALL.
PHOTO BY JOHN GRIESHOP/MLB PHOTOS, 1998

▲ BO KNOWS

BO JACKSON OF THE KANSAS CITY
ROYALS BREAKS HIS BAT ON IMPACT
WITH HIS KNEE. JACKSON WAS THE FIRST
PLAYER TO BREAK HIS BAT THIS WAY
AFTER A STRIKEOUT, BUT IT BECAME
QUITE A FAD FOR AWHILE.
PHOTO BY JOHN TREMMEL/MLB PHOTOS

IN THE SHADOWS
Fans wait in the shadows in the ballpark
at Arlington, home of the Texas Rangers.
Photo by Darren Carroll/MLB Photos, 1996

◄ THE BENDS

THE BAT BENDS FROM THE SHEER POWER OF MARK
MCGWIRE'S SWING. HERE MCGWIRE REPRESENTED
THE OAKLAND A'S IN THE ALL-STAR GAME.
PHOTO BY RON VESELY/MLB PHOTOS, 1992

⋀ IT FLOATS

HALL OF FAMER ROGERS HORNSBY, COACHING
THE ST. LOUIS BROWNS HERE, WAS THE GAME'S
GREATEST RIGHT-HANDED HITTER. HE CAPTURED
SEVEN BATTING CHAMPIONSHIPS AND AVERAGED
BETTER THAN .400 BETWEEN 1921 AND 1925. A
TWO-TIME MVP, HE MANAGED THE 1926 CARDINALS
TO THEIR FIRST WORLD CHAMPIONSHIP.
PHOTO BY NATIONAL BASEBALL LIBRARY/MLB PHOTOS

⋏ ONCE IN A CENTURY
HANK AARON, TED WILLIAMS, AND WILLIE MAYS AT THE
ALL-CENTURY TEAM PRESENTATION BEFORE GAME 2 OF
THE WORLD SERIES. AARON IS THE RBI (2,297) AND
HOME RUN (755) KING, MAYS WAS ONE OF THE GAME'S
GREATEST DEFENSIVE CENTER FIELDERS, AND WILLIAMS
WAS ONE OF THE GREATEST SLUGGERS, BATTING .406
IN 1941. A YOUNG WILLIAMS LOOMS BEHIND THEM.
PHOTO BY RICH PILLING/MLB PHOTOS, 1999

RECORD BREAKER ➤
CAL RIPKEN, JR. OF THE BALTIMORE ORIOLES
ACKNOWLEDGES THE FANS AFTER BREAKING
LOU GEHRIG'S RECORD FOR MOST CONSECUTIVE
GAMES PLAYED, WITH 2,131.
PHOTO BY TOM DIPACE/MLB PHOTOS, 1995

BATTER UP
Ken Griffey, Jr. of the Seattle
Mariners at bat in Baltimore. Griffey's
silhouette is unmistakable. He is a
member of the All-Century Team.
Photo by Jon SooHoo

GOT IT!

ROBIN VENTURA OF THE CHICAGO WHITE SOX
DIVES FOR A BALL DOWN THE THIRD BASE LINE.
PHOTO BY RICH PILLING/MLB PHOTOS, 1998

⋏ GOOD FRIENDS
BABE RUTH EMBRACES LOU GEHRIG ON
LOU GEHRIG DAY IN YANKEE STADIUM,
WHEN GEHRIG, SUFFERING FROM A CRIPPLING
NEUROMUSCULAR DISEASE, TOLD FANS,
"TODAY I CONSIDER MYSELF THE LUCKIEST
MAN ON THE FACE OF EARTH."
PHOTO BY CORBIS/THE BETTMAN ARCHIVES, 1939

GOOD FRIENDS ⋗
FIRST BASEMAN MARK MCGWIRE CHATS
WITH RUNNER SAMMY SOSA DURING THE
MAGICAL SEASON WHEN BOTH PLAYERS
CHASED ROGER MARIS' HOME RUN RECORD.
THE WEEKEND AFTER THIS PICTURE WAS
TAKEN, MCGWIRE WON THE RACE.
PHOTO BY RON VESELY/MLB PHOTOS, 1998

NETTING A WINNER
ALEX DIAZ OF THE SAN FRANCISO GIANTS CAN
ONLY WATCH AS A FAN AT CANDLESTICK PARK
NETS A HOME RUN BALL. THE RUN COUNTED.
PHOTO BY BRAD MANGIN/MLB PHOTOS, 1998

PERFECT PERCH

A FAN OF THE TRIPLE A DENVER ZEPHYRS WATCHES
FROM THE UPPER DECK AT MILE HIGH STADIUM.
PHOTO BY ERIC LARS BAKKE

STIR IT UP
RICKY HENDERSON OF THE OAKLAND A'S
SLIDES INTO THIRD BASE AND GRAIG NETTLES
OF THE NEW YORK YANKEES DURING THE
AMERICAN LEAGUE CHAMPIONSHIP SERIES.
PHOTO BY RICH PILLING/MLB PHOTOS, 1981

◁ LET IT SNOW

JIM LEYLAND, MANAGER OF THE FLORIDA
MARLINS, HITS INFIELD PRACTICE IN THE
CLEVELAND SNOW BEFORE GAME 4 OF THE
WORLD SERIES AGAINST THE INDIANS.
PHOTO BY MICHAEL ZAGARIS/MLB PHOTOS, 1997

△ LAYING DOWN THE LINE

PAINTING THE BASELINE FOR OPENING DAY.
PHOTO BY JOHN REID III/MLB PHOTOS, 1997

EYE ON THE BALL
KEN GRIFFEY, JR. OF THE SEATTLE
MARINERS MAKES A DRAMATIC
CATCH IN CENTER FIELD.
PHOTO BY RON VESELY

TOUGH TACKLE

RAY DURHAM OF THE CHICAGO WHITE SOX
BARRELS INTO SCOTT SERVAIS OF THE CHICAGO
CUBS DURING AN INTERLEAGUE GAME. BOTH
ARE WEARING VINTAGE UNIFORMS.
PHOTO BY RON VESELY

⊰ CELEBRATION

Matt Williams and his San Francisco Giants
teammates greet Kevin Mitchell at the
plate after Mitchell hit a game-winning
home run in the 10th inning to beat the
Cincinnati Reds at Candlestick Park.
Photo by Brad Mangin/MLB Photos, 1990

SLIDING HOME ⋀

Hall of Famer Jackie Robinson slides into
home plate. Robinson, playing here for the
Brooklyn Dodgers, was an electrifying base
runner. In 1947 he became the first African-
American to play in the Major Leagues. He was
voted the National League's MVP in 1949.
Photo by Associated Press

◄ MASKED MAN

JIMMIE FOXX WAS ONE OF BASEBALL'S ALL-TIME
GREAT POWER HITTERS. WHILE HE DID CATCH A
FEW GAMES IN HIS CAREER (WHICH SPANNED
THE 1920S THROUGH THE 1940S), HE USUALLY
PLAYED FIRST BASE. FOXX BELTED 534 HOME
RUNS OVER 20 SEASONS, HITTING 30 OR MORE
IN A RECORD 12 SUCCESSIVE SEASONS.
PHOTO BY NATIONAL BASEBALL LIBRARY/MLB PHOTOS

▲ NOSE TO NOSE

NEW YORK METS PITCHER DENNIS COOK HAS
A WORD WITH HOME PLATE UMPIRE ALFONZO
MARQUEZ AFTER BEING EJECTED IN THE EIGHTH
INNING FROM A GAME AGAINST THE ATLANTA
BRAVES. THE METS WERE PLAYING FOR A WILD
CARD PLAYOFF BERTH IN THAT HEATED GAME.
PHOTO BY MARK LENNIHAN/ASSOCIATED PRESS, 1999

10	R			1	2	3	4
	1	46	SAN FRANCISCO	0	0	3	0
	4	21	COLORADO	0	0	0	
	0	45	CHICAGO (N)	1	0	0	2
	0	10	HOUSTON	0	0	1	0
	5	50	SAN DIEGO				
	6	40	ARIZONA				
	2	25	MC GWIRE	70			
	7	21	SOSA	66			

◁ SIGN OF THE TIMES
ON THE LAST DAY OF THE REGULAR
SEASON, THE SCOREBOARD AT BUSCH
STADIUM IN ST. LOUIS SHOWS THE FINAL
TALLY FOR MARK MCGWIRE AND SAMMY
SOSA'S LEGENDARY HOME RUN DUEL.
PHOTO BY RICH PILLING/MLB PHOTOS, 1998

THE SPLENDID SPLINTER
(PREVIOUS PAGE)
TED WILLIAMS CRACKS YET ANOTHER HIT
FOR THE BOSTON RED SOX. HE WAS THE
LAST PLAYER TO HIT .400 FOR AN ENTIRE
SEASON, WHEN HE ENDED 1941 WITH AN
INCREDIBLE BATTING AVERAGE OF .406.
PHOTO BY THE BREARLEY COLLECTION

<WELCOME HOME
DAVE NILSSON OF THE MILWAUKEE
BREWERS MEETS AND GREETS
A TEAMMATE AT HOME PLATE.
PHOTO BY RON VESELY

SAFE! ʌ
NEW YORK GIANTS THIRD BASEMAN
BOBBY THOMSON STEALS HOME OFF
CINCINNATI REDS CATCHER JOE ROSSI
AT THE POLO GROUNDS IN NEW YORK.
PHOTO BY ASSOCIATED PRESS, 1952

THE BABE AND
THE IRON HORSE

BORROWED RODEO COSTUMES CAN'T DISGUISE
BABE RUTH AND LOU GEHRIG, WHO RODE THIS
LONGHORN INTO THE STADIUM AT AN OCTOBER
EXHIBITION ALL-STARS GAME AT DEXTER
PARK IN BROOKLYN. RUTH WAS ALREADY
RETIRED HERE, BUT GEHRIG STILL PLAYED
FOR THE YANKEES. BASEBALL WAS FULL OF
THESE KINDS OF BARNSTORMING FUN
GAMES, AND RUTH, ALWAYS THE HAM,
WAS A REAL CROWD-PLEASER.

PHOTO BY PACIFIC & ATLANTIC PHOTOS/CORBIS, 1938

BIRD'S EYE VIEW ⋀

VINCE COLEMAN OF THE SEATTLE MARINERS
DIVES BACK TO FIRST ON A PICKOFF ATTEMPT,
AS PAUL SORRENTO OF THE CLEVELAND INDIANS
TRIES FOR THE TAG. THIS PHOTO WAS TAKEN FROM
THE CEILING OF THE KINGDOME IN SEATTLE.
PHOTO BY ROBERT BECK/MLB PHOTOS, 1995

⋖ HE FLIES THROUGH THE AIR

RAY ORDOÑEZ OF THE NEW YORK METS SHOWS WHY
HE IS KNOWN AS ONE OF THE MOST ACROBATIC
SHORTSTOPS IN THE MAJOR LEAGUES.
PHOTO BY AL TIELEMANS, 1998

⋀ OVER AND OUT

HIDEO NOMO OF THE LOS ANGELES DODGERS
SHOWS HIS CLASSIC LONG, TWISTING DELIVERY
ON THE MOUND FOR THE NATIONAL LEAGUE IN
THE ALL-STAR GAME IN ARLINGTON, TEXAS.
PHOTO BY RICH PILLING/MLB PHOTOS, 1995

SPECIAL DELIVERY ➤

DENNIS ECKERSLEY SHOWS HIS SIDEARM DELIVERY
WHILE PITCHING FOR THE CHICAGO CUBS, WHERE HE
PLAYED FROM 1984 TO 1986. ECKERSLEY PITCHED
A NO-HITTER FOR THE CLEVELAND INDIANS, WON 20
GAMES FOR THE BOSTON RED SOX, AND BECAME
ONE OF THE BEST CLOSERS OF ALL TIME WITH
THE OAKLAND A'S. HE WON THE CY YOUNG AWARD
AND AMERICAN LEAGUE MVP IN 1992.
PHOTO BY RICH PILLING/MLB PHOTOS

◁ TURN IT ON

NOMAR GARCIAPARRA, BOSTON RED SOX SHORTSTOP,
CATCHES BRADY ANDERSON OF THE BALTIMORE
ORIOLES AT SECOND AND THROWS TO FIRST,
TRYING TO FINISH OFF A DOUBLE PLAY.
PHOTO BY DAVID L. GREENE/MLB PHOTOS, 1997

EE-YAH ◁

HUGHIE JENNINGS OF THE DETRIOT TIGERS WAS
KNOWN FOR HIS CURIOUS YELL OF ENCOURAGEMENT,
A CONTRACTION OF "THAT'S THE WAY!" BETWEEN
1907 AND 1918 HE MANAGED THE TIGERS AND
ALSO PLAYED IN FIVE GAMES.
PHOTO BY CHARLES M. CONLON/THE SPORTING NEWS, 1910

WHAT IT'S ALL ABOUT

Rawlings is the official ball of Major
League Baseball. There are 108 hand-sewn
stiches on every cowhide ball.

Photo by Robert Beck/MLB Photos, 1998

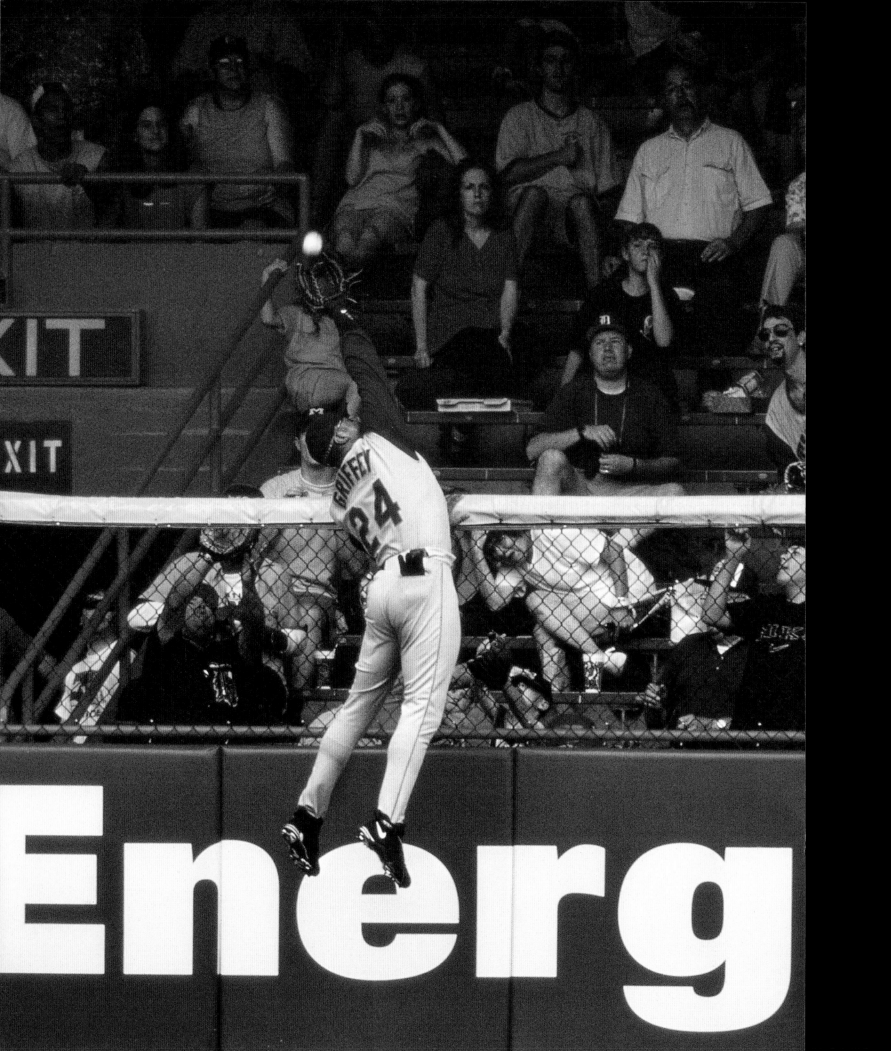

◁ ROBBED!
KEN GRIFFEY, JR. OF THE SEATTLE MARINERS
STEALS A HOME RUN FROM A DETROIT HITTER.
PHOTO BY TOM DIPACE, 1998

EAT DUST ◣
EDDIE PEREZ OF THE ATLANTA BRAVES GIVES A
TEXTBOOK EXAMPLE OF HOW TO BLOCK THE PLATE,
TAGGING OUT A MONTREAL EXPOS RUNNER.
PHOTO BY RICH PILLING/MLB PHOTOS, 1996

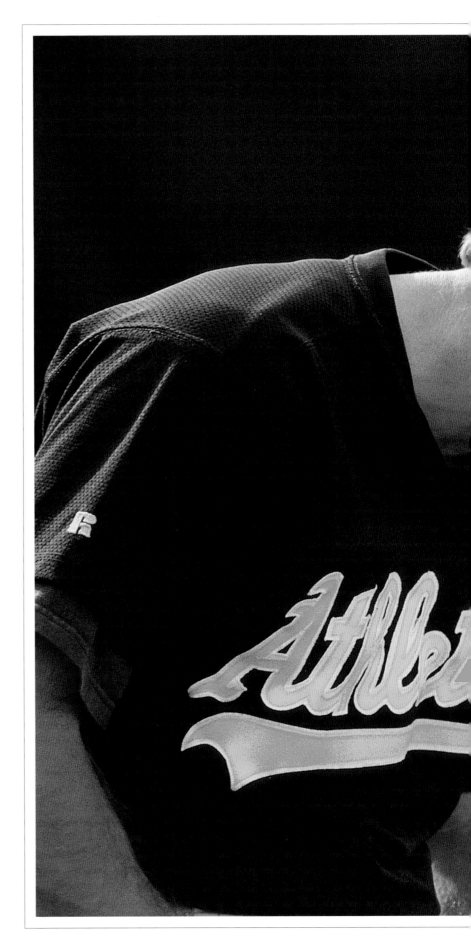

WHEN DAD GOES TO WORK
SCOTT BROSIUS WITH HIS DAUGHTER.
BROSIUS PLAYED FOR THE OAKLANDS A'S
FROM 1991 TO 1997.
PHOTO BY JEFF CARLICK

◄ BIG HANDS
CINCINNATI REDS CATCHER ERNIE LOMBARDI HOLDS
AN AMAZING SEVEN BASEBALLS IN ONE HAND. THE
HALL OF FAMER WAS KNOWN AS "THE SCHNOZ"
BECAUSE HE ALSO HAD A BIG NOSE.
PHOTO BY UPI/CORBIS

FRUIT JUICE ▲
A 21-YEAR-OLD TED WILLIAMS OF THE BOSTON RED SOX
SWATS A GRAPEFRUIT FOR A PHOTOGRAPHER AT SPRING
TRAINING DURING HIS SECOND SEASON. WILLIAMS
LATER SAID HE PREFERRED HITTING BASEBALLS
BECAUSE "THERE'S LESS CHANCE OF GETTING WET."
PHOTO BY WIDE WORLD PHOTOS/AP, 1940

⩓ UP, UP AND AWAY
SANDY ALOMAR, JR. OF THE CLEVELAND
INDIANS LEAPS OVER SEATTLE MARINER KEN
GRIFFEY, JR. IN THIS DANCE AT THE PLATE.
PHOTO BY TONY TOMSIC/MLB PHOTOS, 1994

TWIST AND SHOUT ⩛
PHILADELPHIA PHILLIES THIRD BASEMAN SCOTT
ROLEN MAKES AN AIRBORNE THROW TO FIRST.
PHOTO BY RICH PILLING/MLB PHOTOS, 1998

◄ PERFCT CONTROL

LEROY "SATCHEL" PAIGE, ONE OF THE GAME'S
GREATEST PITCHERS, STARTED OUT IN THE NEGRO
LEAGUES FOR THE KANSAS CITY MONARCHS.
OFFICIAL STATISTICS WERE NOT KEPT, BUT
UNOFFICIAL ESTIMATES ARE THAT HE APPEARED
IN 2,500 NEGRO LEAGUE GAMES AND PITCHED
ABOUT 300 SHUTOUTS, INCLUDING 55 NO-HITTERS.
HE JOINED THE MAJOR LEAGUE CLEVELAND INDIANS
IN 1948 (AT AGE 42), AND WAS ELECTED TO
THE HALL OF FAME IN 1971.
PHOTO BY NATIONAL BASEBALL LIBRARY/MLB PHOTOS

WHO'S NEXT? ∧

CINCINNATI REDS BATTING PRACTICE. THE
BATTING CAGE IS WHEELED ONTO THE FIELD TO
KEEP FOUL BALLS FROM BEING DEFLECTED.
PHOTO BY JOHN GRIESHOP/MLB PHOTOS, 1997

X MARKS THE SPOT
CAL RIPKEN, JR. FORMS THE LETTER X
AS HE REACHES TO MAKE A CATCH.
PHOTO BY BRAD MANGIN/MLB PHOTOS, 1997

◄ OUCH!
RUNNER WALT WEISS OF THE COLORADO
ROCKIES COLLIDES IN THE BASE PATH WITH
MIKE GALLEGO OF THE ST. LOUIS CARDINALS.
PHOTO BY DAN DONOVAN, 1996

WAITING ▲
THE ATLANTA BRAVES DUGOUT
DURING SPRING TRAINING.
PHOTO BY ROBERT BECK/MLB PHOTOS

◁ NEAT AND TIDY

BATS AND BATTING HELMETS STORED IN
THE SHEA STADIUM VISITORS DUGOUT.
PHOTO BY RICH PILLING/MLB PHOTOS, 1994

△ GOOD STRETCH

SCOTT FLETCHER OF THE TEXAS
RANGERS LIMBERS UP BEFORE A GAME.
PHOTO BY LOUIS DeLUCA, 1988

◁ OVER AND UNDER

JEFF BLAUSER OF THE ATLANTA BRAVES GOES
AIRBORNE OVER DELINO DESHIELDS OF THE
LOS ANGELES DODGERS AT SECOND BASE.
PHOTO BY V.J. LOVERO/SPORTS ILLUSTRATED

TWILIGHT TIME ◁

CY YOUNG AWARD WINNER DWIGHT "DOC" GOODEN
OF THE NEW YORK METS THROWS AGAINST THE
SAN FRANCISCO GIANTS AT CANDLESTICK PARK.
PHOTO BY BRAD MANGIN/MLB PHOTOS, 1990

INTO THE BASKET ⋀
CARLOS FEBLES OF THE KANSAS CITY
ROYALS MAKES A CLASSIC BASKET CATCH.
PHOTO BY JOHN WILLIAMSON/MLB PHOTOS, 1999

HEY, HEY WE'RE THE ROCKIES ➤
PREGAME WARM-UPS FOR
THE COLORADO ROCKIES.
PHOTO BY TIM DEFRISCO/MLB PHOTOS, 1995

SLIDE!

RICKEY HENDERSON OF THE SAN DIEGO
PADRES SLIDES INTO HOME AND TOM PAGNOZZI
OF THE ST. LOUIS CARDINALS. THE SAN DIEGO
PLAYER IN THE FOREGROUND GIVES THE
RUNNER THE SIGNAL TO SLIDE.
PHOTO BY DAN DONOVAN/MLB PHOTOS, 1996

◁ ARC AND SHADOW

RYAN CHRISTENSON OF THE OAKLAND A'S PULLS A
BALL BACK FROM OVER THE CENTERFIELD WALL.
PHOTO BY BRAD MANGIN/MLB PHOTOS, 1998

THE HIT ▲

HALL OF FAMER JOHNNY BENCH CONTROLLED
THE GAME ON BOTH SIDES OF THE PLATE WITH HIS
HITTING, THROWING OUT OPPOSING BASE RUNNERS,
CALLING PITCHES, AND BLOCKING HOME PLATE.
PHOTO BY RICH PILLING/MLB PHOTOS

GOT HIM?

RICKEY HENDERSON OF THE OAKLAND A'S TRIES TO AVOID
BEING TAGGED OUT BY THE YANKEE'S RANDY VELARDE.
PHOTO BY LARRY LAMBRECHT/MLB PHOTOS, 1995